THE ROOFUS RULES

12 WAYS TO BETTER LIVE YOUR LIFE THROUGH THE EYES OF A CHIHUAHUA

THE ROOFUS RULES

12 WAYS TO BETTER LIVE YOUR LIFE THROUGH THE EYES OF A CHIHUAHUA

By Anthony Knopps

PALMETTO
PUBLISHING
Charleston, SC
www.PalmettoPublishing.com

Hardcover ISBN: 979-8-8229-3945-5

Paperback ISBN: 979-8-8229-3946-2

Acknowledgements

A book like this wouldn't be possible without the support of family and friends. I don't want to mention any names for fear of leaving anyone out. What started as a fun title with no clear beginning, middle or end, quickly became a tome on how to live a better life. Conversations between my wife, Camille, and me while watching the evening news, with our pet chihuahua within earshot, and continually sharing why people couldn't be more like Roo (Roofus is a pet name when he's being silly, which is often) really drove this idea. I hope you enjoy it as much as we enjoyed creating it.

From Roo

I want to thank you for buying the book that
one of my favorite humans created. I am so glad
he did because I can't type, and my dog words
don't always translate into human ones. Still, I am
glad to be part of this project and even prouder
to be with humans who love me. You see, I was
a rescue. I had several hard early years before a
special girl decided to take a chance on me and
call me her dog. My life has been full of blessings
ever since. I hope you enjoy these rules and make
them a part of your life!

January

BE BRAVE

Don't ever fear starting a new journey. Many times, we
don't know where we will end up, and that's okay. It's
the trip and the growth that comes from the voyage
that makes it worthwhile. After all, a journey you
don't expect can lead to blessings that last a lifetime.
It did for me!

February

BE THANKFUL

Take time to love the little things. Be it a gentle breeze on your skin or discovering a duck on your favorite stream, there is love all around us. It's easy to wallow in our own self-pity and anger. However, when you take the "blinders" off and look around, you may be surprised at what you find. Take the time to pause and notice those special things in life that you might be missing!

March

BE SUPPORTIVE

Celebrate the small events in your day. Be present in the moment, especially moments like these. I love getting hugged by the human who rescued me. Support those who make a difference in your life because it will make a difference in theirs.

April

BE NOT AFRAID

Seasons change and it is how we meet those changes
that reveals what is truly in our heart. Accepting
change leads to growth and growth leads to a fuller
understanding of why we are here. Don't ever
be afraid to embrace that change because what is
outside your window may just be your destiny.

May

BE PREPARED

Not everything goes as planned. Be prepared
for the side trips that you will take on life's
journey because they may lead you to what was
to be your ultimate destination all along.

June

Be Willing

The journey can be long, hard, and tiring. We can never be sure when we are finished. However, we can take solace in the fact that we are improving or at least trying to do so. I see my humans work hard to take care of me. It got me to thinking: If we do one thing better today than we did yesterday, then this day was a success.

July

BE UNPREDICTABLE

Don't be afraid to try new things. It's okay to step
outside of your comfort zone. Be a little silly or
unpredictable by crawling atop your kennel. You
never know what memories you will be creating, both
for you and for your loved ones. Take that chance!

BLUES

August

Be Loving

It's easy to think you are alone in the world. I certainly
did until a special girl found me and took me home.
I learned that it is hard to make time for others, let
alone yourself. However, she taught me that when
we take the time to cherish our friends and family
and make decisions that involve them in our lives,
we come away far richer than when we started.

September

BE POSITIVE

It never seems there is enough time to do what
we set out to do. Instead of getting stuck in the
negative, look at the positive impact you have
made on the lives of your family and the lives
of your friends. Your true self is inside them
and a piece of you is in their every success.

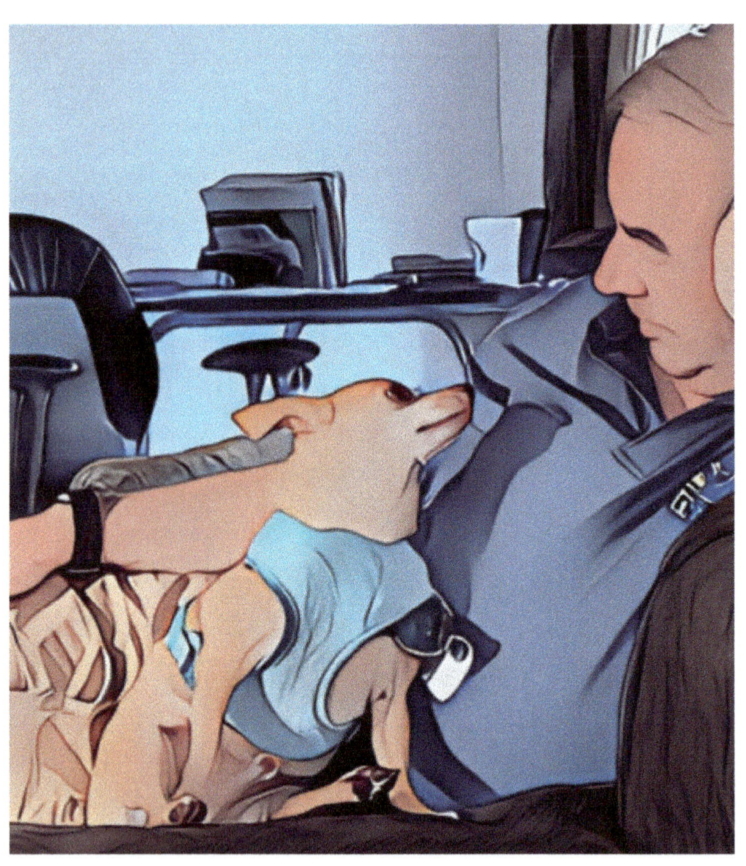

October

BE KIND

It's easy to be angry but so much harder (and important) to forgive and forget. Imagine how our world would be if we took the time to say to others, "we understand" and "what can we do to ease your pain?" A little kindness goes a long way!

November

BE COMMITTED

Each new season is a chance at renewal, not just for those things around you, but for yourself. Take these opportunities to heart and commit yourself to making a difference, both in your life and in the lives of others. Also, try something new and unexpected, such as sledding down the driveway! You may be amazed at how it makes you feel.

December

BE MEMORABLE

There is an end to all things. We must be cognizant of that. The end is not something to fear, but rather something to celebrate. It will be hard for us to say goodbye to the things and to the people we love. It will be incredibly hard on them as well. However, if we make the most of each moment we have with them, it can make the final moment not a reflection of disappointment, but a reflection that makes them smile.

Final Thoughts

Boy, writing a book is hard work!
Once again, I want to thank all of my human friends
and my human family for their never-wavering support
and encouragement as my humans and I worked to
make "The Roofus Rules" a reality. The lessons here
aren't unique, but they serve as a reminder to all of
us to do better, to be better and to be more caring
for those who share the world with us, both humans
and Roofuses—or is that Roofi? I'm not sure!
Seriously, with all of the arguments that are taking
place today in our world, we need to find time to
talk to one another, rather than just talking past one
another. If this book has caused you to rethink how
to approach such things in your daily life or even
to pause and reflect on the beauty that is all around
us, then my humans and I have done our job.
Until we meet again, keep working hard and remember,
it's okay to be a Roofus (in fact, it's encouraged!)